FROM BEING THINGS, TO EQUALITIES IN ALL

JOE MILAZZO

the operating system digital print//document

FROM BEING THINGS, TO EQUALITIES IN ALL

ISBN # 978-1-946031-68-6

edited and designed by ELÆ [Lynne DeSilva-Johnson]

Print books from The Operating System are distributed to the trade by Ingram, with additional production by Spencer Printing, in Honesdale, PA, in the USA. Digital books are available directly from the OS, direct from authors, via DIY pamplet printing, and/or POD.

This text was set in Steelworks Vintage, Europa-Light, Minion, and OCR-A Standard.

Audio for this title, recorded by Joe Milazzo, can be found at
https://soundcloud.com/slow-1/from-being-things-to-equalities-in-all.

Cover Art uses an image from the series "Collected Objects & the Dead Birds I Did Not Carry Home," by Heidi Reszies.

the operating system
www.theoperatingsystem.org
mailto: operator@theoperatingsystem.org

FROM BEING THINGS,
TO EQUALITIES
IN ALL

goes permits in been letting sated some
locking exits into begun before all revisiting

falling given zeroes interceded before often citing
along pulling kidnapped fires against befriended weighing

thinning complements numbered out of teeming
in envisioned following roving loops over shrouded

to now grinning of addressed besides to strengthening sucked amplifying mortified none lessened infesting any

informed off heaved airs up smelters
sublimes into versus earlier arraigning

distinguished forgetting through stalks above studies
tuned mounts marbled under mounted often stripping

ranges ranked paralleled impresses without turned testing thieving commends like clearing in since commixes

doubted stemming at worsened loaning rumored
summoned films occupying minus eating eaten

through clicked beneath seconding setting interests alongside tunneled next spent suiting behind knowing assaulted sums foregoing except asked accepting when near placing compressed of appearing buttressed all deepened billeting

bricks lest mitigating among can prepared bleaches stowed
until drilled first locked around responding last in harmed

guesses sometimes stews roots over reached mouthing
easing angered from invitations up some dustings knives

shining regards righted pointing owing pledges
objected next never arresting for attracted between

illuminated presently soils assured of after hewing
mooring blight warning graying contributed afar feared

freed sugared lasting from traded apiece neutered substituting coming with connoted with flagged

signaling before impressing across lived recognizing
recovering connected reworded upon refuses jacketing

pitted off given negotiated lights throughout asks believing after dived scanning for attempted aside as intimates disrupted

opposing utters infected beyond bled perturbs
rays via saved dressing over named concerning

patterned halting outside out until embraced out availed whitened by not whitening levels contracting

acting all in breathing for fields wrapping reviewed
out of diluting unbounded plus papered gasps polished

crests always of courses amid passes rising busied amounting
in consents biting in spited starred posts in through

inside averted truncated selected among several angling
invading with parts naturalized attaches seldom proposing

spilling coddled down unapplied leaves surfacing
blaring athwart singled honors splitting regarded into

slider grays given like against stolen embodied out holding
slept despite sprawling next improvised beyond recruiting

some tingled per glimpsed moralized despite failing reddening
when over counted amid all exploded few shares telling out

of across cringing seaming naturalized within into excuses
intoxicated hungering of edging rattled near including crosses

wanted   wanting   since   littering   angles   betrayed
around   barring   found   near   until   throws   vacating

transported charges since scrabbling most at echoing
seeming few rippled fronts now until at timing agreed

AFTER-WORDS

REVENANT SYNTAX: THE HALF-FORGOTTEN LANGUAGE OF PERPETUAL WAR

A CONVERSATION WITH JOE MILAZZO

Greetings! Thank you for talking to us about your process today! Can you introduce yourself, in a way that you would choose?

I live and work in Dallas, Texas — a much unloved place — where I was born and raised. I've published three books: a novel and two collections of poetry. To keep body and soul together, I hold down a job in digital marketing (creative and strategy). To put it another way: Monday through Friday, 9 to 5, I lean into the most mediocre aspects of our culture. Doing so has been exhausting and inspiring in equal measure.

Why are you a poet/writer/artist?

I write in order to figure out what it is I'm writing about. (I don't mean to be clever, only succinct.) Writing, for me, is more about the process than the outcome. Specifically, how that process is simultaneously bewildering and clarifying. I guess another way to put it is that I write in order to satisfy my need to improvise.

When did you decide you were a poet/writer/artist (and/or: do you feel comfortable calling yourself a poet/writer/artist, what other titles or affiliations do you prefer/feel are more accurate)?

I grew up around books and have had an interest in literary aesthetics for as long as I can remember. By "literary aesthetics" I mean the total literary experience, from physically handling books to (re)assembling language using the various tools traditionally available to writers. I think of myself as a "language worker." (I have an MLS and have worked as a professional librarian.) I'm increasingly uncomfortable with the notion of authorship, not only because it is cognate with "authority" but also because of its commodification. I also prefer "maker" to artist. The activity matters more to me than the position and the perceived privilege that accompanies it.

What's a "poet" (or "writer" or "artist") anyway? What do you see as your cultural and social role (in the literary / artistic / creative community and beyond)?

A poet is an artist whose primary medium and raw material is language. An artist is someone who has fallen in love with their chosen media and raw materials. By fallen in love I mean: commits a significant amount of their attention to something or someone. To attend to is to care for. So I like the idea of assigning the poet/writer/artist a clerical function, with all the denotations and connotations of that term in a near-constant state of excitement. Writers/poets/artists record, take stock, are members of a professional class. The discipline they follow also requires that they minster to others. To do so most effectively, they have to be centered in their selves (or subjectivities), and achieving as much depends on a certain asceticism.

Talk about the process or instinct to move these poems (or your work in general) as independent entities into a body of work. How and why did this happen? Have you had this intention for a while? What encouraged and/or confounded this (or a book, in general) coming together? Was it a struggle?

This text is my attempt to imagine a post-post-modernist American idiom. Not a future language but a language of the present we might occupy if the past were to be imagined differently. That is, a language purged of deracination and ironizing. A language in which signifiers and signifieds are no longer fundamentally estranged. (This being not so mush reunification as collapse.) A language capable of acknowledging the degree to which it is both private refuge and public domain. A language aware of its situation vis-a-vis history's horizon.

Did you envision this collection as a collection or understand your process as writing or making specifically around a theme while the poems themselves were being written / the work was being made? How or how not?

I tend to work in series. That was true in this instance as well. One of these couplets — I'm afraid I can no longer remember which — seeded the entire text. That is, one of these expressions revealed to me possibilities for elaboration and the potential to become "about" a concern in excess of its own operations. So, if there is a theme here, it is "variations." With the fundamental concept fixed in place, the writing became a matter of exploring what the constraints (see below) latent in that primary expression might generate (or excite).

What formal structures or other constrictive practices (if any) do you use in the creation of your work? Have certain teachers or instructive environments, or readings/writings/work of other creative people informed the way you work/write?

The construction of *From Being Things, To Equalities In All* was guided by syntactical, semantic and graphical constraints. Those constraints included, but were not limited to: a heavy reliance on what readers of English recognize as participles and gerunds (whether they are still participles and/or gerunds here is, I hope, open to interpretation); the imposition of margins; exploitation of the semi-concrete capacities of digital typography; the employment of of what I think of as the revenant language of the first decade of the 21st Century — that half-forgotten language of perpetual (what we now might term normalized) war.

Speaking of monikers, what does your title represent? How was it generated? Talk about the way you titled the book, and how your process of naming (individual pieces, sections, etc) influences you and/or colors your work specifically.

I read the title of *From Being Things, To Equalities In All* as a paraphrase of Thomas Jefferson's so-called "immortal declaration." Or, if not a paraphrase, a self-conscious attempt at meme-ing Jefferson's idea/sentiment. First things often come last (as Joseph McElroy once told me), and that was the case here. Once the text was complete, I realized a needed a title that did what titles traditionally do, only not completely. An expository title. But the exegesis here is slightly out-of-focus (from my point of view, anyway), even as it suggests that a manifesto will shortly be raising its voice.

What does this particular work represent to you as indicative of your method/ creative practice? and/or as indicative of your history, your mission/intentions/ hopes/plans?

This text is probably the most explicitly "experimental" one I've produced. In some sense, it represents allegiances that have weakened since I earned my MFA at CalArts. In another sense, it represents the fulfillment of a certain duty I feel when I set out to write something — to disencumber myself of that voice I may be said to have found for myself, and to explore that vast and coterminous, if not precisely contiguous, territory of "other" vocabularies, grammars, and, I hope, realms of experience.

What does this book DO (as much as what it says or contains)?

Presuming it succeeds, this text achieves the status of rhetoric. It sings with efficacy and an original coherence. It goes so deep into noise that it finds signal where none of us ever expected to encounter any.

What would be the best possible outcome for this book? What might it do in the world, and how will its presence as an object facilitate your creative role in your community and beyond? What are your hopes for this book, and for your practice?

I hope that *From Being Things, To Equalities In All* inspires other language workers to respond to our present state of emergency by attending even more closely — and personally — to the rich contingencies encoded in syntax.

Let's talk a little bit about the role of poetics and creative community in social and political activism, so present in our daily lives as we face the often sobering, sometimes dangerous realities of the Capitalocene. How does your process, practice, or work otherwise interface with these conditions? I'd be curious to hear some of your thoughts on the challenges we face in speaking and publishing across lines of race, age, ability, class, privilege, social/cultural background, gender, sexuality (and other identifiers) within the community as well as creating and maintaining safe spaces, vs. the dangers of remaining and producing in isolated "silos" and/or disciplinary and/or institutional bounds?

Inclusivity isn't just a laudable goal. I believe it imperative to the survival of our species. Unfortunately, however, inclusivity can be exposed as rather defenseless when confronted by what we euphemize as pragmatism. Complicating this fact is how easily we can be distracted by overt displays of ideology. More pernicious, in my experience, is the myth of the meritocracy, an imaginary set of relations promulgated by both art-world gatekeepers and academic celebrities. Our entire system of taste, aesthetic worthiness and artistic accomplishment is so embedded in capitalism… but it becomes very tempting to believe that capitalism is OK, or can be reformed, when it just so happens that the collateral damage it does benefits you (and I include myself in that second person). I'm talking here about conventional definitions of success, yes, but also the expectation to which almost all of us are addicted: that, because making is labor, it can or should sustain us at the material level. Therefore, in the interests of making literature more humane, I think the biggest challenge we face is actually twofold. One, we have dismantle the existing critical discourse and break the sway it has over everything from creative writing pedagogy to the social currency that circulates within our literary communities. In short, no more geniuses, only valences of partiality. Two, we have to find a way to build a system of value upon a foundation of valuelessness. I don't believe that the Maslowian necessity of art needs to be reclaimed — I'm not an atavist or irredentist — but I do believe that, in the interests of providing for the needs of all, we must reckon with the entropic consequences of indifference, broadly conceived. If nothing else, transparency of attention is in order. (Maybe what we need is real market research focused on how how literary influencers learn about, acquire, process and become ambassadors for texts and authors.) Jos Charles and Sesshu Foster have written/spoken much more intelligently on all of these topics than I, and I refer sympathetic readers to the following online resources:

https://www.pw.org/content/ten_questions_for_jos_charles and
https://www.poetryfoundation.org/harriet/2017/08/how-is-the-artist-or-writer-to-function-survive-and-produce-in-the-community-outside-of-institutions .

However, if I were to sum this point up for myself, I would might formulate it thusly: "No more speculation, but only as they say in the auction house, and mean it."

ABOUT THE AUTHOR

JOE MILAZZO is the author of the novel *Crepuscule W/ Nellie* and two collections of poetry: *The Habiliments* and *Of All Places In This Place Of All Places*. He is also an Associate Editor for *Southwest Review*, a Contributing Editor at *Entropy*, and the proprietor of Imipolex Press, a tiny publishing house dedicated to the promotion and preservation of heteronymic literature. Joe lives and works in Dallas, TX, and his virtual location is www.joe-milazzo.com .

ABOUT THE COVER ART:

The Operating System 2019 chapbooks, in both digital and print, feature art from Heidi Reszies. The work is from a series entitled "Collected Objects & the Dead Birds I Did Not Carry Home," which are mixed media collages with encaustic on 8 x 8 wood panel, made in 2018.

Heidi writes: "This series explores objects/fragments of material culture--how objects occupy space, and my relationship to them or to their absence."

ABOUT THE ARTIST:

Heidi Reszies is a poet/transdisciplinary artist living in Richmond, Virginia. Her visual art is included in the National Museum of Women in the Arts CLARA Database of Women Artists. She teaches letterpress printing at the Virginia Commonwealth University School of the Arts, and is the creator/curator of Artifact Press. Her poetry collection titled *Illusory Borders* is forthcoming from The Operating System in 2019, and now available for pre-order. Her collection titled *Of Water & Other Soft Constructions* was selected by Samiya Bashir as the winner of the Anhinga Press 2018 Robert Dana Prize for Poetry (forthcoming in 2019).

Find her at heidireszies.com

WHY PRINT:DOCUMENT?
(AND WHAT DOES THIS MEAN FOR DIGITAL MEDIA?)

The Operating System has traditionally used the language "print:document" to differentiate from the book-object as part of our mission to distinguish the act of documentation-in-book-FORM from the act of publishing as a backwards-facing replication of the book's agentive *role* as it may have appeared the last several centuries of its history. Ultimately, we approach the book as TECHNOLOGY: one of a variety of documents across a range of media that humans have invented and in turn used to archive and disseminate ideas, beliefs, stories, and other evidence of production.

Ownership and use of printing presses and access to (or restriction of) information/materials, libraries, and archives has long been a site of struggle, related in many ways to revolutionary activity and the fight for civil rights and free speech all over the world. While (in many countries) the contemporary quotidian landscape has indeed drastically shifted in its access to platforms for sharing information and in the widespread ability to "publish" digitally, even with extremely limited resources, the importance of publication on physical media has not diminished. In fact, this may be the most critical time in recent history for activist groups, artists, and others to insist upon learning, establishing, and encouraging personal and community documentation practices.

With The OS's print endeavors I wanted to open up a conversation about this: the ultimately radical, transgressive act of creating PRINT / DOCUMENTATION in the digital age. It's a question of the archive, and of history: who gets to tell the story, and what evidence of our lives, our behaviors, and/or our experiences are we leaving behind? We can know little to nothing about the future into which we're leaving an unprecedentedly digital document trail--but we can be assured that publications, government agencies, museums, schools, and other institutional powers that be will continue to leave BOTH a digital and print version of their production for the official record. Will we?

As a (rogue) anthropologist and long time academic, I can easily pull up many accounts about how lives, behaviors, experiences--how THE STORY of a time or place--was pieced together using the deep study of the archive: correspondence, notebooks, and other physical documents which are no longer the norm in many lives and practices. As we move our creative behaviors towards digital note taking, and even audio and video, what can we predict about future technology that is in any way assuring that our stories will be accurately told--or told at all? How will we leave these things for the record?

For all our years of print publication, I've said that "with these documents we say: WE WERE HERE, WE EXISTED, WE HAVE A DIFFERENT STORY", but now, with the rapid expansion of greater volume with digital and DIY printed media, we add: we ARE here, and while we are, we will not be limited in what we add value to, share, make accessible, or give voice to, by restricting it to what we can afford to print in volume.

Adding a digital series is the next chapter of *our* story: a way for us to support more creative practitioners and offer folks independent options for POD or DIY-zine-style distribution, even without our financial means changing -- which means, each book will *also* have archive-ready print manifestations. It's our way of challenging what is required to evolve and grow. Ever onward, outward, beyond.

Elæ [Lynne DeSilva-Johnson]. Founder& Creative Director
THE OPERATING SYSTEM, Brooklyn NY 2019

THE 2019 OS CHAPBOOK SERIES

DIGITAL TITLES:

American Policy Player's Guide and Dream Book - Rachel Zolf
The George Oppen Memorial BBQ - Eric Benick
Flight Of The Mothman - Gyasi Hall
Mass Transitions - Sue Landers
The Grass Is Greener When The Sun Is Yellow - Sarah Rosenthal & Valerie Witte
From Being Things, To Equalities In All - Joe Milazzo
These Deals Won't Last Forever - Sasha Amari Hawkins
Ventriloquy - Bonnie Emerick
A Period Of Non-Enforcement - Lindsay Miles
Quantum Mechanics : Memoirs Of A Quark - Brad Baumgartner
Hara-Kiri On Monkey Bars - Anna Hoff

***

PRINT TITLES:

Vela. - Knar Gavin
[零] A Phantom Zero - Ryu Ando
Don't Be Scared - Magdalena Zurawski
Re: Verses - Kristina Darling & Chris Campanioni

***

DOC U MENT

/däkyəmənt/

First meant "instruction" or "evidence," whether written or not.

noun - a piece of written, printed, or electronic matter that provides information or evidence or that serves as an official record
verb - record (something) in written, photographic, or other form
synonyms - paper - deed - record - writing - act - instrument

[*Middle English, precept, from Old French, from Latin documentum, example, proof, from docre, to teach; see dek- in Indo-European roots.*]

Who is responsible for the manufacture of value?

Based on what supercilious ontology have we landed in a space where we vie against other creative people in vain pursuit of the fleeting credibilities of the scarcity economy, rather than freely collaborating and sharing openly with each other in ecstatic celebration of MAKING?

While we understand and acknowledge the economic pressures and fear-mongering that threatens to dominate and crush the creative impulse, we also believe that ***now more than ever we have the tools to relinquish agency via cooperative means,*** fueled by the fires of the Open Source Movement.

Looking out across the invisible vistas of that rhizomatic parallel country we can begin to see our community beyond constraints, in the place where intention meets resilient, proactive, collaborative organization.

Here is a document born of that belief, sown purely of imagination and will.
When we document we assert. We print to make real, to reify our being there.
When we do so with mindful intention to address our process,
to open our work to others, to create beauty in words in space,
to respect and acknowledge the strength of the page we now hold
physical, a thing in our hand… we remind ourselves that,
like Dorothy: *we had the power all along, my dears.*

THE PRINT! DOCUMENT SERIES

is a project of

the trouble with bartleby

in collaboration with

the operating system

www.ingramcontent.com/pod-product-compliance
Lightning Source LLC
Chambersburg PA
CBHW030135100526
44591CB00009B/670
9781946031686